THE LIBRARY OF
nutrition™

Food Labels
Using Nutrition Information to Create a Healthy Diet

Rose McCarthy

rosen
central™

The Rosen Publishing Group, Inc., New York

Published in 2005 by The Rosen Publishing Company, Inc.
29 East 21st Street, New York, NY 10010

First Edition

Library of Congress Cataloging-in-Publication Data

McCarthy, Rose.
Food labels: using nutrition information to create a healthy diet / by Rose McCarthy.—1st ed.
     p. cm.— (The Library of nutrition)
Includes bibliographical references and index.
ISBN 1-4042-0300-1 (library binding)
1. Food—Composition—Juvenile literature. 2. Nutrition—Juvenile literature.
3. Food—Labeling—Juvenile literature.
I. Title.
TX551.M1456 2005
664—dc22
                                                          2004015538

Manufactured in the United States of America

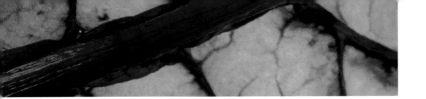

contents

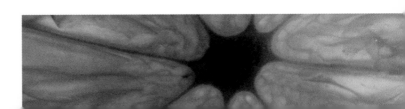

introduction

At first glance, the nutrition label required by the federal government to appear on food packages does not look like particularly interesting reading. It is filled with measurements, percentages, and technical terms that are usually not found outside of a science book. But take a closer look. Food labels contain information that could help you create and maintain a healthy diet. In turn, changing the way you eat can have substantial health benefits that will change the way you feel.

America is facing an "obesity epidemic." Too many people are eating too much of the wrong types of foods, and more than half of all Americans have become over-weight or obese as a result. Bookstores are heavily stocked with books promoting miraculous and rapid diet plans that promise maximum and speedy weight loss with minimal effort. Meanwhile, many people have overlooked the valuable dietary guidelines that are provided for free on most food packaging: food labels.

Reading food labels requires some basic background knowledge of nutrition. Once the specialized terms, the various vitamins and minerals, and the nutrition categories (such as fats, carbohydrates, and proteins) are understood, it becomes easy to read any food label and quickly gather

A shopper reads the food label on a container of yogurt. Many brands of yogurt use high-fructose corn syrup as a sweetener, which some nutritionists believe can lead to weight gain, high blood pressure, and heart disease.

the relevant and important information it provides. Food labels enable people to track and, if necessary, limit their intake of calories, fat, sugars, and other nutrients throughout the day. However, using this wealth of information to create a healthy diet requires dedication.

Dedication to a balanced diet and a healthy lifestyle is worth the effort. The combination of exercise and good eating habits not only lowers

Teenagers exercise at a YMCA in Olathe, Kansas, as part of a program that aims to fight childhood obesity.

the risk of obesity, it also reduces your chances of developing cancer, heart disease, and a number of other medical conditions linked to obesity and aging. Staying in good physical shape makes people feel better about themselves and improves the likelihood of living a long, healthy life. A clear understanding and active use of food labels can act as valuable tools toward achieving these health goals.

chapter 1

The History of the Food Label

The United States Food and Drug Administration (FDA) is the government agency charged with protecting public health by assuring the safety, usefulness, and security of prescription drugs, medical devices, cosmetics, and our nation's food supply. The FDA also promotes public health by providing members of the American public with accurate, science-based information they need to use medicines and foods to improve their health.

The FDA established the first food-labeling guidelines in 1938 as part of the Federal Food, Drug, and Cosmetic Act. This legislation required packaging labels to list the food's name and weight as well as some information about the company that produced the food. Manufacturers could include any other information that they thought might persuade shoppers to buy their products.

Though this law represented a major step forward in an era when very little was known about basic nutrition, the new labels still did not reveal very much about the actual contents of the packages. In some cases, they did

SHAKE BEFORE SERVING

Nutrition Facts

Serving Size 1 can (340mL)

Amount Per Serving

Calories 70   Calories from Fat 0

% Daily Value*

Total Fat 0g	0%
Saturated Fat 0g	0%
Cholesterol 0mg	0%
Sodium 980mg	41%
Total Carbohydrate 14g	5%
Dietary Fiber 2g	8%
Sugars 10g	
Protein 2g	

Vitamin A 80% (80% as Beta Carotene)

Vitamin C 140% • Calcium 4% • Iron 10%

*Percent Daily Values are based on a 2,000 calorie diet. Your daily values may be higher or lower depending on your calorie needs.

	Calories:	2,000	2,500
Total Fat	Less than	65g	80g
Sat Fat	Less than	20g	25g
Cholesterol	Less than	300mg	300mg
Sodium	Less than	2,400mg	2,400mg
Total Carbohydrate		300g	375g
Dietary Fiber		25g	30g

New, improved, and standardized food labels, like this one on the side of a can of tomato juice, were required by the government to appear on nearly all food and drink packaging beginning in 1994.

not even list the product's ingredients. Most Americans knew nothing about vitamins, minerals, nutrients, or the three main food substances—carbohydrates, proteins, and fats. Nor did they know of the specific value of these dietary elements and their recommended daily intake. Instead, parents generally encouraged their children to eat as much food as they could—whatever it might be—so they would grow big and strong.

Grocery store shelves have changed dramatically since the 1930s, and so have shoppers. This shift has much to do with researchers' increasing understanding of the role of diet and nutrition in physical health. Once experts began to realize that our diets directly impact our health, they began to recommend limits on fat, sugar, salt, and cholesterol—all dietary elements that we require but that become harmful in excessive amounts. As more Americans became interested in balanced diets in the 1970s and 1980s, new laws gradually required food manufacturers to list more detailed and useful information on their food labels.

The Need for a New Food Label

Companies began including more nutrition information on packaged foods, but the labels were often more confusing than informative to shoppers. Food manufacturers began to use labels to make questionable health claims rather than provide consumers with useful facts about what the products contained. Food companies targeted health-conscious consumers by adding labels such as "light," "reduced fat," "low in cholesterol," or "heart healthy." These claims were often misleading. For instance, a packaged dinner might boast that it contained less than a gram of sodium, leading the buyer to believe that it was a low-sodium product. In reality, however, most people need less than a gram of

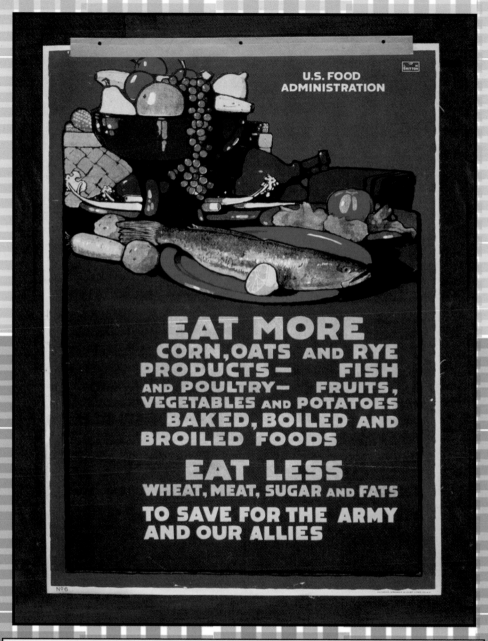

In an attempt to both improve Americans' diets and support wartime rationing, this World War II–era FDA poster encourages a diet similar in many ways to today's recommendations of whole grains, fruits, vegetables, fish, and chicken over high-fat and high-calorie red meat, sweets, and fats.

sodium in an entire day, much less in a single meal. The government had no guidelines to regulate these kinds of misleading claims.

Consumers were also puzzled by the inconsistency and lack of standardization among food labels of various products. Serving sizes were not standardized, which made it difficult to compare the nutritional value of different brands. When one brand of ice cream listed a smaller serving size than another, its calorie, fat, and sugar count also appeared to be smaller, even though it might actually be higher in calories, fat, and sugar than its competitor. Companies often listed

The Food Watchdogs

Responsibility for regulating foods in the United States belongs to two government agencies, the Food and Drug Administration and the United States Department of Agriculture (USDA). The USDA inspects meat and poultry products to ensure that they are safe and labeled accurately. It is also responsible for the inspection and weighing of grain. The FDA makes sure that foods are produced and processed in safe, sanitary conditions. Both agencies work to promote consumer safety and awareness.

The manufacturer of these pork rind snacks tries to capitalize on the current low-carb diet trends by advertising its protein product as containing "zero carbs."

very small serving sizes in order to make their foods appear to be low in calories, even though they knew most consumers would eat servings larger than what was recommended.

Congress and the FDA Take Action

By the late 1980s, many consumers no longer trusted the claims they read on food labels. Organizations concerned with health and diet, such as the American Dietetic Association and the American Heart Association, also voiced their concern over inadequate food labels. As a result, in 1990, Congress passed the Nutrition Labeling and

FDA commissioner David Kessler, who served under U.S. presidents George H. W. Bush and Bill Clinton, testifies before the Senate on regulating vitamin manufacturers' claims.

Education Act (NLEA), authorizing the FDA to improve and expand food labels. Under Commissioner David Kessler, the FDA also began investigating and halting some of the food industry's deceptive labeling practices.

Kessler believed that standardized food labels should be required on most packaged foods. The FDA would strictly define what qualified as "low fat" and "reduced sodium" to prevent deceptive labeling. Health claims—such as "foods high in fiber prevent heart disease"—would have to be scientifically proven before they could be printed on a package. The FDA would also standardize the portion sizes of particular

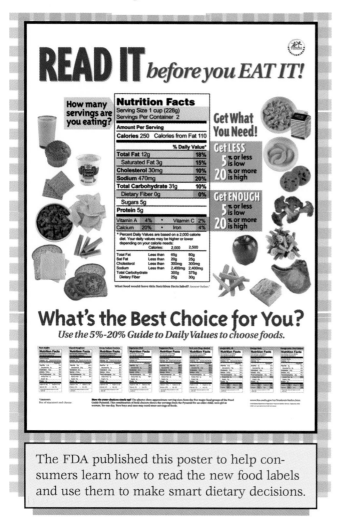

The FDA published this poster to help consumers learn how to read the new food labels and use them to make smart dietary decisions.

kinds of food, such as potato chips, cookies, soups, and breakfast cereals.

Consumers and food manufacturers both supported the plan, hoping to end shoppers' confusion and frustration in grocery store aisles. The FDA now faced the challenge of reviewing all previous food-labeling guidelines to produce a single straightforward and informative label. Further complicating this task, the FDA also had to coordinate its efforts with the United States Department of Agriculture (USDA), another food regulatory agency. In November 1991, the two agencies released a 600-page report on the proposed new food label.

Food companies objected to some of the strict requirements in the new rules. To label a product "reduced fat," for example, the FDA wanted the manufacturers to cut fat content by 50 percent, a more significant reduction than manufacturers were willing to make. After reviewing manufacturers' complaints, the FDA compromised on some of the new rules. "Reduced fat" foods now only have to contain one-third less fat than the original product, even if that represented less than a 50 percent reduction. Initially strict requirements for "reduced sugar" and "reduced salt"

 **FACT!**

Under an early version of the food-labeling rules, even candy could be labeled as a "healthy" food. The FDA later fixed this loophole with a law called the "jelly bean rule."

labels were also loosened during the FDA's review of its proposed rules.

President George H. W. Bush approved the revised food label report in 1992. The FDA then publicly issued the 875-page finalized version of the new food label requirements in early 1993. Food companies were given more than a year to comply with the new labeling standards. Manufacturers estimated that the new labels would cost $600 million.

chapter 2

Overview of the Food Label

In the spring of 1994, newspaper headlines and television talk shows alike turned their attention to the new food-labeling regulations, while food companies hurried to meet the government's deadline. Though a few people criticized the new rules for not being strict enough, most praised the improvements over the old labeling system. Meanwhile, the FDA focused its energies on educating Americans about the new labels and the new kinds of helpful information they contained.

The first obvious improvement to the food label was its size and organization. Before 1994, ingredients and nutrition information could be printed in very small type anywhere on the package, in no particular order. The new label includes a large rectangular box with the heading "Nutrition Facts." Within this new format, each piece of nutrition information appears in a specific order, with the most important information listed first—serving size, servings per container, calories, fat, cholesterol, sodium, carbohydrates, and protein. Because this format is the standard, shoppers can easily compare the labels of two brands of cereal, for example, and quickly determine which contains more calories, fat, sugar, and so on.

Serving Sizes

Serving sizes are also standardized and set at reasonable snack- or meal-sized portions. Most products list the volume or amount of a serving—one cup of pasta, a slice of bread, one-eighth of a packaged cake—as well as its weight, measured in grams and milligrams. The serving size for foods such as condiments (ketchup, mustard, salsa) or fats is usually quite small, measured in tablespoons or teaspoons. A serving of salad dressing, for example, is one to two tablespoons, a serving of butter is one tablespoon, and a serving of sugar is a teaspoon.

While a sandwich can make for a very nutritious lunch, the meal can be made more healthy by substituting juice for soda and baked chips or carrot sticks for fried potato chips.

Serving sizes for some foods are set at a single unit. Therefore, a hamburger at a fast-food restaurant counts as a single serving. In this way, customers can compare the nutritional information of hamburgers at Burger King, Wendy's, and McDonald's even though the burgers vary in size and weight from one restaurant to the next.

Percent Daily Values

Besides listing the serving size, the new labels also indicate how the food fits into a balanced daily diet. The amount of nutrients found in each serving is listed underneath the serving size. These include calories, fats, cholesterol, sodium, carbohydrates, proteins, vitamins A and C, calcium, and iron. Labels also give a "Percent Daily Value" for each of these nutrients. This figure tells how much of a person's daily requirement for each nutrient is provided by a single serving of the food. The Percent Daily Values are based on amounts set by the FDA. For instance, a healthy diet should generally not include more than about sixty-five grams of fat. A single serving of potato chips (about eleven chips) might contain ten grams of fat, equal to 15 percent of the FDA's recommended daily fat intake. Because only eleven chips go a long way toward a person's daily fat intake, that person would have to carefully choose what he or she eats during the rest of the day, in order to avoid going well over the FDA's suggested limit.

Conversely, food labels also point out which nutrients you will need more of to stay healthy. The FDA recommends at least ninety milligrams per day of vitamin C. The serving of chips might provide 8 percent of the recommended daily intake (or seven mg), meaning that someone eating a handful of chips will need to get at least eighty-three milligrams more of vitamin C from other sources.

Scientific Health Claims

An old proverb claims, "An apple a day keeps the doctor away." Traditional kitchen wisdom states that chicken soup is the best cure for a cold. The FDA, however, requires scientific proof of a product's benefits before it will allow the manufacturer to place health claims on its labels.

Manufacturers can only mention a connection between a food product or nutrient and the reduced risk of a medical condition in a few specific cases. For example, calcium has been linked to healthy bone density (thickness and strength). Saturated fat and cholesterol are known to increase risk of coronary heart disease. Evidence suggests that a high-fiber diet may lower the risk of some types of cancer. As a result, food products that are rich in calcium, high in fiber, or low in cholesterol and saturated fats can make the appropriate health claims. Altogether, the FDA recognizes about fourteen of these types of health claims in which certain ingredients or nutrients are clearly linked with specific health benefits.

In general, nutritionists have concluded that a healthy diet includes plenty of fiber, fruits, and vegetables, and limited amounts of sodium, fat, and cholesterol. If their products fit the FDA's criteria, food manufacturers may try to attract buyers by labeling their product "fat free," "sugar free," "low sodium," or "high in fiber." The FDA specifies standards for each term. Products "free" of fat, cholesterol, sodium, sugars, or calories can have only an extremely tiny amount per serving. The FDA defines certain benchmarks for products to qualify as "low," "high," "good source,"

In response to the low-carb diet craze, food producers are creating new versions of their products. These Pecan Delights candy bars are now available in original, sugar-free, and low-carb varieties.

FACT!

Vitamin and mineral supplement containers are labeled with "supplemental facts" similar in format to the nutrition facts panel on packaged food.

"reduced," "less," "light," and "more" in nutrients or calories. Meat, poultry, and seafood low in fat and cholesterol can be labeled "lean" or "extra lean." A separate regulation prohibits misleading claims; a food must be a good source of a nutrient or ingredient for the nutrient and its corresponding health claim to be highlighted on the label. So, for example, a product that contains a small amount of oat bran cannot claim to be a good source of fiber. It cannot even claim something like "made with oat bran," because consumers might be tricked into thinking the product was a significant source of oat bran.

Exceptions to the Rules

Several types of food are exempt from nutrition labeling. Most notably, restaurant food generally does not have to be labeled. The FDA only requires restaurants to provide nutrition information if they make a content claim—such as "low fat"—for a dish on their menus. Some fast-food restaurants voluntarily provide customers with nutrition information on their menu offerings. They often provide nutrition information pamphlets at the restaurant or post the information on their Web sites.

Bakeries, delis, hot-dog stands, and some other food vendors are also exempt from labeling. Food shipped in bulk and some foods with no nutrients, such as coffee and tea, also do not have to be labeled. Labeling for most fresh food is voluntary. Rather than requiring grocery stores to label each apple or pack of pork chops, the FDA encourages sellers to post nutrition information somewhere in the store.

Further Improvements to the Food Label

In 2003, the FDA added trans fats to its food-labeling requirements. Trans fats are found in foods such as vegetable shortening, some margarines, crackers, candies, baked goods, cookies, snack foods, fried foods, salad dressings, and many processed foods. Most forms of trans fats are generally produced by turning liquid oils into solid fats. Scientific studies have shown that trans fats (along with the better-known saturated fats) raise cholesterol levels in the body, and therefore increase the likelihood of coronary heart disease. Starting in 2006, food companies will be required to list trans fat on labels.

Food labels could be a valuable tool in curbing America's "obesity epidemic"—results of the 1999–2000 National Health and Nutrition

Labeling Organic Foods

Most food available today is produced with the help of manufactured chemicals. Farmers use herbicides, pesticides, and chemical fertilizers to increase crop yields (the size of a harvest). Antibiotics and steroids are fed to farm animals—such as cows, lambs, and chickens—to protect  them from disease, fatten them up, and increase their production of milk and eggs. People concerned about the health risks of eating food containing such chemicals have the option of choosing organic foods produced without artificial or manufactured chemicals. The USDA's National Organic Program, effective since October 2002, standardized labeling for organic foods. Today, organic foods bear labels stating that they are "100% organic," "organic," or "made with organic" products.

Examination Survey (NHANES) report that more than 60 percent of U.S. adults are overweight and 30 percent are obese. If all foods displayed nutrition information, some believe, Americans would be more aware of the nutritional content of what they eat. They might then make smarter decisions about what they eat and reduce their portion sizes. In particular, it has been proposed that all restaurants be forced to provide nutrition information for each of their dishes. Restaurants often attract customers with rich food and large portions. If customers were told of the nutrition content of items on a menu, they might be more likely to make healthy choices. The FDA has also considered making calorie count and serving size information on food labels easier to find and read.

Some experts have advised the FDA to review its guidelines on the recommended daily intake of vitamins and minerals. The current recommendations rely on data from 1968. To determine the appropriate daily allowances, the FDA used the highest value needed by any segment of the population (usually growing boys) rather than the value needed for the average individual. Most Americans do not require the levels of vitamins and minerals as high as the current recommendations. However, other critics worry that if the daily values were revised,

Freshly cut sugarcane is being loaded onto a railroad car to be sent to a mill where it will be refined into white granulated sugar.

President George W. Bush's FDA commissioner, Mark McClellan, points to an enlarged reproduction of a food label while announcing the new requirement that trans fats be listed on the Nutrition Facts panel.

food companies might reduce the amount of vitamins and minerals in their foods.

Health experts and organizations have also urged the FDA to include on nutrition labels the amount of sugar added to foods. The FDA advises people to consume sugar in moderation, though it has not set an official daily recommended value for sugar. In 2003, the World Health Organization recommended that sugar should make up less than 10 percent of a person's daily diet. Food companies in the United States strongly objected. Because of their strong influence on nutrition guidelines, it is unlikely that added sugar will appear on food labels. Nutrition experts recommend trying to consume less than 40 grams (about 10 teaspoons) of added sugar per day. One 12-ounce can of soda contains 12 teaspoons of sugar.

chapter 3

The ABCs of Nutrition

Food labels make nutrition information easily accessible, but the labels are more meaningful and useful if you have some basic knowledge of nutrition. Poor nutrition can increase your chance of developing cancer, heart disease, diabetes, vitamin and mineral deficiencies, and other medical conditions. A well-balanced diet can reduce the risks of disease and improve one's quality of life.

Counting Calories

Human beings eat in order to survive. The human body produces energy by breaking down the food it ingests. Calories are a measure of the energy contained in food. To maintain a healthy weight, we must consume the same number of calories that we burn through exercise and everyday activities.

The number of calories per serving of food, listed directly below the serving size, is one of the most important numbers on a food label. By keeping track of calories throughout the day, you can determine whether or not you are eating the

24

appropriate amount of food for your dietary needs. Food labels assume that the typical American requires 2,000 calories a day, but caloric requirements vary from one person to another. Most people need an amount somewhere between 1,600 and 2,800 calories. Men generally require more calories than women. Because they are growing—a process that requires enormous amounts of energy—children and teenagers require more calories than adults. Most people need fewer calories per day as they age. Men and women with active lifestyles

As little as thirty minutes of moderate exercise per day will burn enough calories to help you maintain a healthy weight.

need more calories than sedentary (non-active) people who do not burn as much energy through exercise or an otherwise busy daily routine.

Food labels also list the number of calories from fat per serving. Most Americans consume more fat than advised by nutritionists, and this figure makes it easy for shoppers to avoid products high in fat.

Know Your Nutrients

Below the caloric content, food labels list nutrients and their daily values in percentages. The human body relies on nutrients for metabolism (the conversion of food into energy), growth, and basic functions. Nutrients are divided into two categories. Macronutrients, usually measured in grams, include protein, fat, carbohydrates, and water. Micronutrients, usually measured in milligrams or even smaller units, include vitamins and minerals. A balanced diet provides adequate amounts of both macronutrients and micronutrients.

Of the macronutrients, most nutritionists agree that people should get between 50 and 60 percent of their calories from carbohydrates, 10 to 20 percent from protein, and less than 30 percent from fat. Food labels can help people choose healthy forms of these three groups.

Fats

The first macronutrient to appear on food labels is fat. A food's total fat and saturated fat contents are both listed. Soon the label will also list "Trans Fat." Some food companies voluntarily list two additional types of fat—polyunsaturated fat and monounsaturated fat. Many dieters believe that fat should be avoided whenever possible, but it is not that simple. Some types of fat are more healthy than others and have actually been proven to reduce the risk of heart disease.

While it is no surprise that doughnuts, cookies, and peanut butter are high in fat, other foods we think of as healthy—such as some brands of granola, energy bars, and wheat crackers—can also be high in both fat and calories.

Dietary fats affect cholesterol levels in the blood. Cholesterol is a steroid alcohol in body fluids that keeps membranes fluid, but which can also cause clogging of the arteries, which leads to heart attacks. High levels of low-density lipoproteins (LDL), the so-called bad cholesterol, can increase the risk of heart disease. High-density lipoproteins (HDL), the good cholesterol, actually help protect the heart. Saturated fat and trans fat raise bad cholesterol levels and lower good cholesterol levels. Polyunsaturated and monounsaturated fats raise good cholesterol levels and reduce bad levels.

No more than 10 percent of your caloric intake should come from saturated fat. Some nutritionists recommend less than 5 percent. Foods high in saturated fat include whole milk and red meat. You should also limit foods high in trans fats, such as margarine, vegetable shortening, and products deep-fried or baked with trans fats. Instead, look for products that replace saturated and trans fats with oils high in monounsaturated and polyunsaturated fats, such as olive oil, peanut oil, or corn oil.

Cholesterol

Cholesterol is the macronutrient listed next on food labels. This category refers to dietary cholesterol consumed in food, which is different from the cholesterol naturally produced in the body. Experts recommend consuming no more than 300 milligrams daily. Plants do not produce cholesterol, so it is found only in meat, poultry, fish, and dairy products.

 FACT!

Not all foods are equal in terms of calories. A gram of protein or carbohydrates has four calories. A gram of fat has nine calories.

When fatty substances, such as cholesterol, build up in the arteries (as seen above), a blockage can result. Blocked arteries result in reduced blood flow and can deprive the heart of oxygen, leading to a heart attack.

Carbohydrates

Under "Total Carbohydrate"—the third macronutrient listed on the label—appear the subcategories of "Dietary Fiber," "Sugars," and sometimes "Sugar Alcohol" and "Other Carbohydrate." Fiber, which can only be found in plant-based foods, aids digestion and can help lower cholesterol. "Sugars" include both naturally occurring sugars (like those found in fruit) as well as added sugars such as white or brown sugar, corn syrup, honey, maltose, fructose, and so on.

Most carbohydrates come from plant foods—fruits, vegetables, and grains. Fruits and vegetables are an important natural source of vitamins and minerals, and they can reduce the risk of many medical conditions, including heart disease and various cancers. Experts advise eating a variety of fruits (two to four servings) and vegetables (three to five servings) every day.

Some carbohydrates from grains have more nutritional value than others do. Whole grains, such as brown rice, barley, and oats, are lower in fat and better sources of vitamins, minerals, protein, and fiber than

white bread or white rice, for example. Look for products made from whole grains, such as whole-grain cereal or whole wheat and multigrain bread and pasta. Avoid grains that are low in fiber and that provide few vitamins and minerals, especially refined carbohydrates that list white flour or corn syrup as the main ingredient. Instead of turning to a "low carb" plan that probably will not ensure an adequate and balanced diet, choose healthy carbohydrates and count calories. For a person who requires 2,000 calories per day, about 1,000 to 1,200 should come from carbohydrates.

Bread, pasta, and rice are all good sources of carbohydrates. Whenever possible, choose whole-grain breads and pastas and brown rice over white varieties.

Empty Calories

Some foods contain calories but do not provide nutrients or any extra benefits such as fiber. Many desserts, candies, and snack foods contain little more than empty calories. Many Americans have diets that include too many of these empty calories. Therefore, people can be malnourished even when  they eat plenty of food or are obese. They simply make the wrong food choices and do not consume an adequate amount of nutrients. Reading labels can help people become aware of whether their food contains anything other than sugar, fat, and calories.

Protein

Protein is the final macronutrient listed on the food label. The human body uses dietary protein to build new cells and maintain tissues. Most people get their protein from animal products such as meat, poultry, fish, eggs, and dairy products. Beans and nuts also contain significant amounts of protein. The average individual needs to consume about eight grams of protein per twenty pounds of body weight daily. Since that is a relatively small amount, few Americans, not even vegetarians, are likely to suffer from a protein deficiency. Vegetarians must be sure to eat a wide variety of fruits, vegetables, grains, and beans in order to be sure that they are getting all of the eight essential amino acids. Unlike meat proteins, plant-based proteins do not each contain all eight amino acids, so they must be combined in order to create a "complete" protein. Food labels do not list a percentage daily value for protein.

Vitamins and Minerals

Vitamins are natural substances that are found in both plants and animals. Minerals are substances that originate in rocks and metal ores. Plants obtain minerals from the soil in which they grow, and animals, including humans, absorb these nutrients when they eat plants.

Food labels list the minerals sodium and sometimes potassium beneath cholesterol. Sodium is a component of sodium chloride, or table salt. It is an electrolyte—a mineral that helps

Though red meat often gets the most attention, beef is not the only good source of protein. Chicken, fish, pork, lamb, beans, nuts, and eggs also provide protein and are often healthier options than beef.

maintain the balance of fluids in the body. Adults generally require about 2,400 milligrams of sodium daily. Sodium is a flavor enhancer of food, however, and for that reason most people consume far more than they need. Excess sodium has been linked to high blood pressure. Potassium, another electrolyte, is found mainly in fruits and vegetables. Unlike sodium, most healthy people have no need to limit potassium in their diets.

Food companies are also required to include on labels the amounts of vitamin A, vitamin C, and the minerals calcium and iron that are found in a single serving of the food product. Labeling of other vitamins and minerals is optional.

Vitamin A, also called retinol, plays an important role in vision, bone growth, infection fighting, and regulation of the immune system. Liver, whole milk, eggs, and butter are high in vitamin A. Carrots, can-taloupe, broccoli, and some other fruits and vegetables contain beta-carotene, which the body can convert into vitamin A.

A daily diet that includes several servings each of a variety of fruits and vegetables will provide your body with many of the vitamins and minerals it needs to function properly and stay healthy.

Although scientists do not fully understand how vitamin C works, it is known to help the body fight infection and stimulate the immune system. Citrus fruits, green peppers, and other fresh fruits and vegetables are the best sources of vitamin C.

Calcium is the mineral present in our bodies that builds bones and teeth. Since dietary calcium is necessary to maintain the strength of these bones, it is very important for growing children and teenagers to consume the recommended amount of calcium. Most adults need about 1,000 milligrams daily, but youths and women may require 1,200 to 1,500 milligrams. Women build less bone mass than men and lose it at a faster rate as they grow older.

Iron is mainly used by red blood cells to carry oxygen throughout the body as part of the respiratory cycle. Most people require at least eighteen milligrams of iron per day to avoid a deficiency. An iron deficiency causes a condition called anemia, in which the number of red blood cells decreases and the body gets less oxygen than it needs, resulting in very low energy. Because women lose so much iron during their monthly period, they are more likely than men to become anemic. As a result, women often require more iron then men. On the other hand, too much iron—especially in the form of iron supplements—can also cause health problems, such as heart disease, colon cancer, and diabetes. Food such as beef, chicken, tuna, and egg yolks are excellent natural sources of iron. Some plant foods also contain iron, including fruits, spinach, and iron-fortified breads and cereals.

chapter 4

Using Food Labels to Create a Balanced Diet

Most Americans recognize the importance of a nutritious diet, but they often have trouble following through on plans to choose healthier foods. When people have the time to prepare home-cooked meals, they often pick easy and familiar dishes rather than experiment with new recipes that might be healthier. Easier still is popping a prepackaged frozen dinner into the microwave or ordering Chinese takeout. Plus, many people do not want to give up their favorite foods for "healthy" alternatives that they fear may be bland or taste bad.

When trying to create a balanced diet, you might feel frustrated at first as you try to sort out all of the information listed on food labels. Keeping track of nutritional content will gradually become an automatic, effortless habit, however. As you become more familiar with the serving sizes and nutrients of various foods, you will not even need to check food labels every time you want to have a snack or prepare a meal. You will know that information without having to refer to the packaging.

Though eating out or buying prepared foods might seem like the best option when you are too hungry or tired to cook, it can have many drawbacks. It will probably cost more, you cannot control the portion size, and the ingredients and preparation might make the meal high in calories and fat.

Packing the Perfect Lunch

Good nutrition starts with an examination of your daily diet and how it could be improved. Let's take a look at a typical brown-bag lunch, including a sandwich, a soda, a thermos of soup from a can, a bag of potato chips, and a packaged ice cream treat purchased at the cafeteria. By checking food labels, you can learn which foods are high in fat and calories and choose healthier alternatives.

Use whole-grain bread for the sandwich. If you are a fan of peanut butter and jelly, try to buy natural peanut butter. Peanut butter is a good

The nutritional value of school lunches can vary greatly. While the student on the right eats a healthy salad, the student on the left has ordered a high-fat cheeseburger and tater tots.

source of protein, but it is high in calories, and some manufacturers add saturated fat and sugar. Almond and cashew butters are also delicious and healthy. Choose a low-sugar jam or jelly, or try a natural fruit spread such as apple or pumpkin butter. Experiment with different healthy combinations. For example, a lot of people like peanut butter and banana sandwiches.

Instead of a sandwich made with deli meat such as bologna, use freshly cut lean chicken or turkey. Processed meat often contains large amounts of fat, salt, and preservatives and has less protein than nonprocessed meats. Try skipping high-fat spreads like mayonnaise, or substitute them with mustard or low-fat mayonnaise. Instead of low-nutrient iceberg lettuce, add high-nutrient romaine lettuce or fresh spinach to your sandwich. Most types of soda are high in calories and contain few nutrients. Grab a juice box labeled "100 percent juice" or a serving of low-fat milk instead. These both contain fewer calories and more nutrients, and milk is a good source of calcium. If you absolutely cannot give up soda, look for the lower-calorie diet versions of your favorite brands.

Some varieties of canned soup can be both healthy and tasty, though many are high in sodium. Look for soups that claim to be "low sodium" or "sodium reduced." A "fat free" label is also a bonus.

Many types of potato chips are deep-fried and contain few nutritional benefits. For a healthier chip, pick a variety that is baked, rather than fried, and check the label for low-fat and low-sodium readings. Look for more nutritious options, perhaps plain popcorn, pretzels, or baked corn chips. Even better, consider healthy alternatives to packaged snacks. Pack your favorite raw vegetables, such as carrots and celery sticks, slices of green pepper, or pieces of broccoli and cauliflower. Grab fresh fruit or a fruit cup. If you choose canned fruit, check the label to see that it is packed in water, not sugar syrup, which is high in calories due to the added sugar. Include a small cup of low-fat cottage cheese or a hard-boiled egg. Experts used to advise people to limit eggs because of their high cholesterol content. More

FACT!

You don't need to feel too guilty about enjoying chocolate! Chocolate contains plant compounds called flavanoids. These flavanoids are also found in tea, cranberries, strawberries, peanuts, and apples. They keep blood pressure down and prevent blood clots and clogging of the arteries.

recently, however, nutritionists have looked at the benefits of eggs—which are high in protein, vitamins, and some polyunsaturated fats—and determined that it is safe for most people to eat an egg a day.

After you read the label on the ice cream, you may opt for a lighter dessert! Packaged ice cream bars generally contain at least 250 calories and a significant amount of saturated fat. Some brands contain more than 400 calories and include 100 percent of the daily recommendation for saturated fat. Ice cream, cakes, cookies, and other sweet desserts are often packed with calories, fat, and sugar. Consider limiting yourself to half of a serving, such as one or two small cookies or a small square of carrot cake. Better yet, choose an alternative to rich desserts. Add fresh strawberries or blueberries to a small carton of yogurt. Stir cinnamon into a serving of applesauce. Mix together a handful of dried fruit, unsalted nuts, and a few chocolate or carob chips to create a homemade trail mix.

Reading the Ingredients

Food labels include one very important section in addition to information on nutrients: the ingredients. Ingredients are listed in descending order by weight. If you are trying to decide between two similar brands or if you cannot tell from the nutrients list whether the food is healthy, take a look at the ingredients. For example, you might want to skip a cereal that lists sugar rather than bran as its first ingredient or a pack of tortillas that is made with white flour rather than cornmeal. Some people also choose to avoid products made with the flavor enhancer monosodium glutamate (MSG), artificial sweeteners, artificial colors, some preservatives, and other additives that may pose health risks. As a general rule, purchase foods that contain the same sorts of basic natural ingredients that you cook with at home.

Conclusion

A healthy diet and plenty of exercise can help build the foundation for a healthy lifestyle. Too many Americans develop poor eating habits during childhood and carry them into their adult years. Obesity in youth, if not treated, can lead to serious health problems during adulthood. Many people try to lose weight with fad diets and begin an unhealthy and ineffective pattern of "yo-yo dieting." By educating yourself about nutrition and using food labels, you can form healthy habits that will last a lifetime.

Food labels should be seen as guidelines, not as inflexible rules. Human beings eat for survival, but we also eat for pleasure, enjoying tasty food and good company at the dinner table. It is OK to occasionally enjoy a rich slice of cheesecake or a batch of fried onion rings. Food labels can help us decide which foods should make up the core of our diet and which types of foods we should minimize and treat ourselves to only occasionally.

This does not mean that a well-balanced diet is limited and uninteresting. On the contrary, most nutritionists agree on the importance of eating a wide variety of foods, especially fruits and vegetables. A healthy diet also provides both long-term and short-term health benefits. If you consume the correct amount of nutrients, you are less

Creating a more nutritious diet does not have to be a solitary struggle. Get your whole family involved in the effort to make better food choices. Together, you can make healthy eating both easy and fun.

likely to suffer from vitamin or mineral deficiencies, obesity, and obesity-related conditions, such as diabetes. Decades in the future, your healthy eating habits may help protect you from cancer and heart disease.

When you pick up a box of food to check the label, encourage your friends and family also to learn about food labels and the importance of proper nutrition. It is never too late to change unhealthy eating habits, and you can set an example for those around you. The food label might not be great literature, but it could contain some of the most valuable information that you and your loved ones will ever read.

Glossary

calcium A mineral important to the makeup of most plants and animals. In humans and animals, it helps build and strengthen bones.

carbohydrate An essential structural part of living cells and source of energy for animals.

cholesterol A substance found in animal tissues and some foods that is used in building cell tissues. In humans, it can build up in the arteries, causing dangerous blockages.

coronary heart disease A condition in which blood flow to the heart is restricted by cholesterol buildup in the arteries.

electrolyte A mineral that regulates some metabolic processes.

fiber Coarse, indigestible plant matter.

herbicide A chemical that kills plants (such as weeds) or interferes with their growth.

high-density lipoproteins (HDL) A form of cholesterol that travels easily through the bloodstream and is associated with a decreased risk of coronary heart disease; often called "good cholesterol."

low-density lipoproteins (LDL) A form of cholesterol associated with a greater risk of coronary heart disease; often called "bad cholesterol."

minerals Inorganic substances found in nature and vital to the nutrition of plants, animals, and humans.

monounsaturated fat An oil or fatty acid that may reduce the levels of LDL cholesterol.

obese Excessively overweight, generally 20 percent over one's ideal body weight.

pesticide A chemical used to kill or discourage insects and other pests.

polyunsaturated fat An oil or fatty acid that may help reduce blood cholesterol levels.

potassium A nutritionally valuable mineral commonly found in salts that assists in muscle contraction and in maintaining fluid and electrolyte balance in body cells. Potassium is also important in sending nerve impulses as well as releasing energy from protein, fat, and carbohydrates during metabolism (the breaking down of food into energy).

saturated fat A fat or fatty acid that is solid at room temperature and has been linked to increased risk of coronary heart disease.

sodium A mineral found in salt that possesses nutritional value and in humans regulates the balance of fluids, the contraction of muscles, and the sending and receiving of nerve impulses.

trans fat An unhealthy substance that is made when food manufacturers turn liquid oils into solid fats by adding hydrogen (in a process called hydrogenation). Trans fat can be found in vegetable shortenings, some margarines, crackers, cookies, snack foods, and other foods made with or fried in partially hydrogenated oils.

vitamins Any of a group of organic substances essential to the nutrition of most animals and some plants. They are present in food and sometimes produced in the body, but they do not provide energy.

For More Information

American Dietetic Association
120 South Riverside Plaza, Suite 2000
Chicago, IL 60606-6995
(800) 877-1600
Web site: http://www.eatright.org/Public

Food and Nutrition Information Center (FNIC)
Agricultural Research Service, USDA
National Agricultural Library, Room 105
10301 Baltimore Avenue
Beltsville, MD 20705-2351
(301) 504-5719
Web site: http://www.nal.usda.gov/fnic

National Institutes of Health (NIH)
9000 Rockville Pike
Bethesda, MD 20892
(301) 496-4000
Web site: http://www.nih.gov

U.S. Department of Agriculture (USDA)
Food and Nutrition Service
3101 Park Center Drive, Room 926
Alexandria, VA 22302
Web site: http://www.fns.usda.gov/fns/default.htm

U.S. Food and Drug Administration (FDA)
Center for Food Safety and Applied Nutrition
5600 Fishers Lane
Rockville, MD 20857
(888) INFO-FDA
Web site: http://vm.cfsan.fda.gov/list.html

Web Sites

Due to the changing nature of Internet links, the Rosen Publishing Group, Inc., has developed an online list of Web sites related to the subject of this book. This site is updated regularly. Please use this link to access the list:

http://www.rosenlinks.com/linu/fola

For Further Reading

Cheung, Lilian. *Be Healthy! It's a Girl Thing: Food, Fitness, and Feeling Great.* New York: Crown Publishers, 2003.

D'Amico, Joan, and Karen Eich Drummond. *The Healthy Body Cookbook: Over 50 Fun, Active, and Delicious Recipes for Kids.* New York: John Wiley & Sons, 1998.

Kowtaluk, Helen, and Alice Orphanos Kopan. *Food for Today.* New York: Glencoe/McGraw-Hill, 2000.

Leedy, Loreen. *The Edible Pyramid: Good Eating Every Day.* New York: Holiday House, 1996.

Nissenberg, Sandra K., ed. *The Healthy Start Kids' Cookbook: Fun and Healthful Recipes That Kids Can Make Themselves.* New York: John Wiley & Sons, 1998.

Rockwell, Lizzy. *Good Enough to Eat: A Kid's Guide to Food and Nutrition.* New York: HarperCollins Publishers, 1999.

Salter, Charles A. *The Nutrition-Fitness Link: How Diet Can Help Your Body and Mind.* Brookfield, CT: Millbrook Press, 1993.

Sears, William, M.D., Martha Sears, R.N., and Christie Watts Kelly. *Eat Healthy, Feel Great.* New York: Little, Brown, and Co., 2002.

Shanley, Ellen, and Colleen Thompson. *Fueling the Teen Machine.* Palo Alto, CA: Bull Publishing, 2001.

Warner, Penny. *Healthy Treats and Super Snacks for Kids.* New York: McGraw Hill Companies, 1994.

Bibliography

Gorman, Christine. "The Fight Over Food Labels." *Time*, July 15, 1991: 52–56.

Jordan, Peg, R.N. *How the New Food Labels Can Save Your Life.* Studio City, CA: Michael Wiese Productions, 1994.

Martin, Andrew. "Panel Urges FDA Alter List of Daily Nutrients." *Chicago Tribune*, December 12, 2003: A1.

Nestle, Marion. *Food Politics: How the Food Industry Influences Nutrition and Health.* Berkeley, CA: University of California Press, 2002.

Rinzler, Carol Ann. *Nutrition for Dummies.* Foster City, CA: IDG Books Worldwide, Inc., 1997.

U.S. Food and Drug Administration. "The Food Label." FDA.gov. May 1999. Retrieved June 2004 (http://www.fda.gov/opacom/ backgrounders/ foodlabel/newlabel.html).

Weil, Andrew, M.D. *Eating Well for Optimum Health: The Essential Guide to Food, Diet, and Nutrition.* New York: Alfred A. Knopf, 2000.

Willett, Walter C., M.D. *Eat, Drink, and Be Healthy: The Harvard Medical School Guide to Healthy Eating.* New York: Simon & Schuster, 2001.

Index

About the Author

Rose McCarthy is a freelance writer living in Chicago, Illinois.

Photo Credits

Cover (background images), back cover images, title page (background images), pp. 3, 4, 7, 16, 24, 34, 39 © David Wasserman/Artville; cover image, p. 1 © Ryan McVay/Getty Images; pp. 5, 6, 11, 12, 19, 21, 22, 23, 36 © AP/World Wide Photos; pp. 8, 26, 28, 29 © Custom Medical Stock Photos; p. 10 © Prints and Photographs Division/Library of Congress; p. 13 © Terry Ashe/Getty Images; p. 14 courtesy of the Food and Nutrition Service of the Department of Agriculture/Department of Health and Human Services/Food and Drug Administration; p. 17 © Steve Prezant/Corbis; p. 25 © Richard T. Nowitz/Corbis; p. 30 © Peter Guttman/Corbis; p. 31 © Royalty-Free/Corbis; p. 32 © Agricultural Research Service/United States Department of Agriculture; p. 35 © Banana Stock/Superstock; p. 40 © Ariel Skelley/Corbis.

Designer: Geri Fletcher; **Editor:** John Kemmerer